Dedicated to Tamara, Aaliyah and the children of the world. You are the true inspiration behind this book. May you be forever happy, enlightened and kind towards all living things.

YASMINE HAMMAD

BLOSSOMING KINDNESS

AUSTIN MACAULEY PUBLISHERS™

LONDON * CAMBRIDGE * NEW YORK * SHARJAH

Copyright © Yasmine Hammad (2020)

ISBN – 9789948356202 – (Paperback)
ISBN – 9789948356196 – (E-Book)

Application Number: MC-10-01-2964961
Age Classification: E

The age group that matches the content of the books has been classified according to the age classification system issued by the National Media Council.

First Published (2020)
Austin Macauley Publishers FZE
Sharjah Publishing City
P.O. Box: 519201
Sharjah, UAE
www.austinmacauley.ae
+971 655 95 202

Foreword

Kindness is a catalyst for solving the world's biggest problems. Through our research, at Kindness.org, we've found that kindness has the power to significantly impact well-being. We use this and other learnings to motivate people around the world to take action because each kind act, small or large, matters.

We believe a kinder world is possible because everyone has the capacity to be kind. It transcends difference and is universal, and *Blossoming Kindness* reminds us just how many opportunities we have each day to choose it. Regardless of the background, race, gender, social status or age, we are capable of cultivating tolerance, empathy and compassion with our kind behaviours. Grandpa Hadid and his grandchildren are the greatest examples showing that kindness is a universal act and not region specific or background focused.

Team Kindness, kindness.org

Praise for Blossoming Kindness

"Our children need to know they are loved, they are safe, they are worthy and they are good enough. Yasmine's book shows kids their inner magic and importance. I am a huge supporter of wisdom that can translate beyond words, borders and boundaries of any kind, to the children of this world. If you have children, work with children or simply love children, get this book for them."
Ariane de Bonvoisin — Best-selling Author of Giggles and Joy; Speaker, Entrepreneur, Coach.

"In 'Blossoming Kindness' lies a great gift for a parent: a simple, effective and important tool to teach children about kindness, empathy, compassion, understanding and acceptance, through a tale that is engaging, relatable and absolutely delightful. Yasmine has created characters that our children will want to emulate and befriend, and what better way to learn about kindness than to see it manifested in others we admire? If, as a parent, you want to bolster your child's innate kindness, then this is the book to get that done. 'Blossoming Kindness' teaches that kindness is important, provides ideas on how to practice caring for others and encourages kids to consider the perspective and struggles of the people around them. What a gift to give our children!"
Hala Khalaf — Journalist, Author and Mother.

"The stories are heartfelt."
Jacqueline Way — Founder of 365give, Canada.

"This is simply beautiful. Not only are the words encouraging, enlightening and fulfilling; it also shows that simple things in life are free and it's about creating adventures and how spending quality time together results in deep connections."
Danielle Wilson Naqvi — Mum of 3 and Founder of ZB Foundation.

"It is of such great importance to have your kids start seeing and practicing different acts of kindness from a young age. This kid-friendly book will help you start early."
Irini Girgis — Parent and Child Coach, Kids Summit.

"What a lovely book 'Blossoming Kindness' is! Kindness is beautiful energy and it is contagious. When we all learn to use kind words, kind thoughts, kind acts, everyone will be living in harmony, happily, and peacefully. As the late Dr. Masaru Emoto said, it is the best to educate 'Love and Gratitude' to all children on earth because then they will be adults in 10 to 20 years, and they will make the world a peaceful place. 'Blossoming Kindness' is such a beautiful book to teach children to be kind to self and to others! Thank you so much for making this book! I hope all children will learn to be kind from this book."

With Love and Gratitude, Michiko Hayashi — Ambassador and Global Director, Non-profit organization, Emoto Peace Project
Tokyo, Japan.

Acknowledgements

Putting this story together would not have been possible without the love, patience and support of the following:

My baba and mama for their continuous care and kindness that they have shown me throughout the years. My beautiful sisters, Dalia, Bassant, Mazaher, Reham and Miral, who manage to send me their blessings and positive energy, each in their own special way. My endless gratitude goes to Y. El Sadat, M. Eissa, A. Hundal and A. Salim for their enthusiastic and honest review of the stories (over and over again). I am forever in awe of their valuable feedback and for their unwavering belief in me.

This work wouldn't be complete without mentioning a few memorable acts of kindness that have forever been engraved in my memory:

Tamara (8 years old): When I judged someone in their absence, she defended them, explaining, "Mum, you shouldn't judge, she had to work hard to provide for her family, please be kind with your thoughts."

Aaliyah (7 years old): For her constant concern for street cats, from feeding and nursing them to bringing them in. Always cuddling them like babies and asking, "Can we take him/her home to look after it?"

Taofiq (9 years old): In the middle of writing this book, I read a draft to Taofiq at bedtime and to express his admiration, he said, with eyes half closed, "It is so kind of you to write this book, I hope *Blossoming Kindness* gets published and that all the kids in the world can read it."

Mia (7 years old): Her endless kindness towards her friends is always inspiring. During playdates, she is always eager to share her toys, favourite dolls and her own clothes with other girls.

Youssef (4 years old): Ended a game, when he saw that the boys were getting rough, to protect a girl who is twice his height and age.

Selim (7 years old): His random heartfelt notes to both his parents to remind them how much he loves them.

Haya (13 years old): Stood with her girlfriend when she was being bullied in school and showed unconditional kindness and support when it mattered the most.

Prologue

For an entire week, every summer, I spend joyful quality time with my grandchildren. Lucky me! My first granddaughter, Nayyirah, is thirteen years old, Adam is ten and Milly is nine. This year, we've got a new addition to the summer break crew. That would be Ty, he's eight.

"Ty wasn't very keen on the idea of spending a whole week with an old man and three other children," his mother told me. "He prefers his own company and his toys."

I knew right then that I might have a challenge on my hands, but he's family, so I'm still happy to have him stay with me so we can all get to know him better.

My first favourite thing about spending time with my grandchildren is that we get the chance to explore activities together without having parents telling the children what to do and how to behave. My second favourite thing is that they're a true source of inspiration. At 64, I'm kind of old. But, even at this age, I am still learning how to be aware, true to myself and my surroundings. Many of these lessons are taught to me by my grandchildren.

My name is Grandpa Hadid and I've written this journal so that I can always remember the highlights of the time we've spent together in the summer of 2018. Perhaps — if someone reads this someday — they'll be inspired by my grandchildren's blossoming kindness. They really do have such wonderful souls.

FAMILY BLESSINGS

Our first day together is always really remarkable. We spend time around the breakfast table, over locally baked bread and cheese, trying to catch up with what we've been doing over the past year and talking about our achievements.

This year, Nayyirah kick started it all, telling us that she'd taken on meditation.

"It relaxes me," she explained, "and keeps me focused, happier and calm during the day."

While Nayyirah isn't very keen on studying, she is very focused on peace of mind and the wellbeing of all. She's always trying to find ways to help other people and animals. She makes me super proud and continuously inspires me to be a better person.

"I wrote a short story about a bunch of animals who use artificial intelligence to hunt down their prey and I'm in the middle of finishing the artwork," Adam revealed next.

He is wonderfully creative and genuine and loves using his imagination. Bedtime stories together are my favourite, especially when he sits so close to me and reads them in his softly spoken voice.

Milly revealed that she'd joined the neighbourhood Wheelchair Basketball team.

"I worked so hard to get in, practicing every day," she told us. "I kept visualising myself in the court playing, until my dream became a reality."

A confident young girl, Milly has never allowed challenges to stop her from achieving what she really wants in her life. We could all learn from her persistence and unstoppable determination; I know I do.

The children looked up at me expectantly. Clearly, it was my turn.

"I managed to read 50 books this year," I said. "I also went camping with my brother. We spent quality time catching up and reminiscing about our lives when we were younger. I was young once, you know!" The children laughed.

"I've been looking forward to our week together," I added. "I consider this time spent with you to be a major achievement. The fun–filled memories we make together mean so much to me."

It was Ty's turn to tell us about his year. He was busy playing with his toy car. Thunder, I think he calls it.

"I have nothing to share," he said, looking up uneasily. "Just the normal stuff. You know, school, friends and family. It's all fine. Nothing as exciting as any of your stories."

I felt a bit concerned about him not wanting to share much but I nodded with an accepting smile. I understand that he didn't really want to come on this holiday in the first place. *He'll warm up*, I thought to myself.

Today, what amazed me most about my grandchildren (apart from them being much taller than the last time I saw them!) is the way they so touchingly listened to each other, with their excited young faces clearly showing surprise and compassion.

NOTE TO SELF: There are many ways to show kindness towards the people we love whether they are direct family members or our guardians. My grandchildren taking one week out of their year to spend with me is, to me, an extraordinary act of kindness.

FOR THE LOVE OF ANIMALS

The next day was really hot. We'd made plans to wash my dear old car that we'd be using to journey to and from our adventures throughout the week. All the children were pretty happy to help, except for Milly. She believes that washing cars wastes plenty of water. Eventually coming around, she asked us, "Could you please use only half a bucket of water for the whole wash? You know, so we don't waste water…" We all agreed, even though we didn't think it would actually be possible.

While we were outside, Adam spotted the neighbours' little boy playing with his dog, a beautiful Husky.

"Grandpa, don't you think that dog looks hot?" he asked me, pointing over at him. I had to agree. He was panting heavily and really did seem to be overheating. Adam loves animals, so he called the child over and offered to cool the dog down with water.

He looked at Milly before starting, and I immediately realised why; he was seeking her approval to use the water we'd put aside to wash the car. She recognised his look too and nodded gently.

"Go ahead," she said. "It won't be a waste if you're helping an animal. Please just use the clear water from the bucket, and we'll finish Grandpa Hadid's car with a damp towel."

As I suspected, Ty was hiding behind the car, not at all keen on this washing-the-dog business. He'd been chased by a stray dog when he was four, and the experience had left him traumatised. As a result, he wasn't fond of most animals. Nayyirah gently tapped his shoulder and smiled.

"It's okay if you don't want to help wash the dog," she said, "but would you like to feed him? Dogs love people with food!" Ty nodded, although he still looked a little worried.

Nayyirah went back inside the house and came out with a bowl of shredded chicken and handed Ty the bowl.

"Go on," she said. "You can do it."

Ty took a small step towards the dog (who we found out later was called Duke) and smelling that chicken-flavoured goodness. The dog jumped up, tongue out, licking Ty on the cheeks and begging for the food. At first, Ty was scared but he soon started giggling. We all did. We were so relieved to see him handling the situation so well. As soon as Ty put the bowl down on the ground though, he was back to Mr Serious. *Baby steps,* I thought to myself.

As you can imagine, the dog was pretty happy after that. Cooled off with a full belly, he ran home, with the neighbour's child close behind. It was getting hotter, so I made my way to the front gate to fix the bird feeder that the children had put together last year before the noonday sun came out in full force. Adam came to join me, excitedly pointing out an ant colony he'd just spotted. The other children came closer to observe the undivided army-like line of ants, whilst helping steer Milly's wheelchair to avoid crushing their beautiful assembly.

I thought to myself how ants are a magnificent example of teamwork, harmoniously working together to bring food to the colony. We should learn from them.

"Did you know that even though the ant is smaller than our fingernails, it can miraculously lift 20 times its own body weight and carry it back to the colony?" Adam said excitedly, adding, "I just love ants." All the children were amazed by that piece of information, which made them even squat to get a closer look at this unbreakable formation.

I remember when I was young, I used to push the ants into my jar with a stick and take them back home to see who collected more; seriously, what was I thinking back then?! Now I know better, thanks to these children, to not harm animals or any creatures for that matter.

Little did they know that as they were admiring the ants' line-up, I was admiring their thoughtfulness and compassion towards animals.

NOTE TO SELF: Showing kindness, empathy and compassion towards animals – regardless of what they are, what they look like or how big they are – is a wonderful quality that anyone can develop with trust and time.

STRANGERS ON THE ROAD

The following day, with a half-washed and half-wiped car, we drove out to see a newly released local Sci-Fi movie and have lunch at our favourite spot, an outdoors restaurant with mesmerising views of the mountains.

On our way there, Nayyirah sat next to me in the front, while Adam was sketching the characters for his book in the back, and Milly was admiring the view from the back window. The car ahead of us was driving slowly, hitting brakes every few seconds and not allowing me to pass. I could see Ty getting impatient, so was I. We didn't want to be late for the movie.

"Will you move it, please?!" Ty shouted. At that point, I was pretty irritated too and I pressed hard on the gas pedal and got way too close to the back of the car that we almost crashed into it. I heard Milly squealing with fear at the back as the car moved out of the way at the last minute, allowing us to pass.

There was an icy silence in the car, and then Nayyirah said in an annoyed voice, "Grandpa Hadid and Ty, the person you got angry with, could have been a lost old lady, a scared new driver or a mum with a crying baby in the back. Maybe next time you should think before honking and shouting at someone on the road. You never know what's going on in their car."

It hit me then that she was absolutely right, and I was ashamed. At the next traffic light, I slowed down and pulled over, waiting for the slow driver to arrive. I wanted to make things right and offer the driver my help.

I waved the car down, and when it had safely stopped, I approached the driver's window.

"My apologies for honking at you earlier," I said to the driver, a young lady looking a bit worried.

"Do you need any help?" I asked.

Tool Box

She replied, "That's very thoughtful of you. My front right tyre is flat, and I am on my way to the garage to check on it. I hope I didn't slow you guys down."

I smiled and shook my head. "Not at all. I'm happy to lend a hand in changing it, if you like."

She accepted, and I asked Ty if he'd like to join me as he was going through a serious car phase and I thought he might want to help with checking on the tyre. We got the tools out the back of our car and went straight to hers.

Ty and I were busy changing the tyre when he looked at me and said, "I think Nayyirah was sort of right about not getting angry with someone without knowing the real reason behind their behaviour." He smiled cheekily before adding, "I'm kind of glad we stopped to help though. Changing tyres is pretty rad."

I smiled and handed him the wrench. "Here, use this to tighten that bolt, and promise me that you'll help people in need whenever you get the chance."

He nodded and smiled back.

Thanks to Nayyirah, I don't think Ty and I will ever assume the worst about a slow driver on the road — or anyone else for that matter — ever again. And yes, we miraculously found a decent parking spot at the movies and only missed out on a few minutes of the beginning.

NOTE TO SELF: It's not fair to make assumptions about strangers based on their actions. Try to be kind with your thoughts and give people the benefit of the doubt; you never know what kind of day they're having.

YOU AND YOUR BODY

Adam enjoys helping out in the kitchen. This morning he woke up earlier than the other children to pick fresh fruits and vegetables in the backyard and whip up a homemade breakfast. When I came into the kitchen, I was excited to see him beating eggs for me to cook the omelettes on the stove. Omelettes are my favourite. Seeing me, he said, "Grandpa, I also picked some flowers for the girls. I'm going to put them in a vase on the table." I couldn't help but smile as I started cooking the eggs.

Adam was in such a rush to get the table ready before the children came in, when he unintentionally tripped on the edge of the carpet, dropping the plates and the vase on the floor. They were all smashed into pieces.

"Are you okay?" I called out to him.

He nodded his head sadly.

"I can never finish anything properly. I'm so foolish! Sorry for breaking your plates, Grandpa Hadid."

Before I was able to say another word, Milly came in. She'd seen what had happened from the door. "You know, Adam," she said, "you don't need to be so hard on yourself. Accidents happen all the time. Look at me, I am in a wheelchair and I have accidents every day! Just last night I rode over Ty's toes when I was practicing for my next basketball game!"

She winked at Adam, and we spied just the hint of a smile at the corners of his lips.

Milly added, "I always remember to be kind to myself first though. We can get Grandpa Hadid more plates."

Just then, Ty walked in, followed by Nayyirah who was doing her morning meditation session. "She's right, you know," Ty said. "Driving on my toes kind of hurt, but it was a mistake. Just like this was an accident. Don't worry about it. It's not the end of the world. I will help you clean up."

For someone who had been so timid for the first few days, Ty was suddenly opening up pleasingly and gradually to all of us. I was so delighted.

Nayyirah smoothly asked, "What were you doing up so early anyway?"

"I was trying to make you all breakfast," Adam said. "I even picked you flowers." He pointed at the daisies lying on the table.

"Well, your good intentions are noted, and they count for a lot. We're really grateful. Thank you, Adam!"

Adam smiled. "Well, I'm happy to finish breakfast with Grandpa if you can all wait a bit?" Everyone nodded. "Yes, please!" they said in a chorus.

"Ty and I will help you clean this up," I added. "Please do carry on and don't forget to put the daisies out! I have a water jug you can use. Breakfast won't be complete without the blessing of freshly picked flowers."

Seeing Ty getting involved and offering Adam kind words and hands was quite enjoyable. He might have been disinterested in spending time with us when he first arrived, but his heart is definitely in the right place. I think he really is warming up now.

NOTE TO SELF: Kindness is an energy exchange that starts inside you and spreads to others. Speak to your mind and your body with kindness; they are always listening.

CO-EXISTING IN THE UNIVERSE

We had a lazy day at home today, and Milly forced — or should I say persuaded — us to watch short documentaries about water. I was extremely interested in finding out more about water to figure out Milly's ultimate passion and cause for preserving water.

The series of documentaries that we watched varied between experiments and struggles to save the water resources. The one documentary that caught their attention was called 'Water has memory', which shows that water has memory and can even save information in the same way a computer does. On top of that, water's structure can actually be affected by human emotion! Interesting, right?

Various experiments were performed by scientists around the world, specifically Dr Masaru Emoto, a Japanese scientist. He revealed a deeper understanding of water by observing the physical effect of words, prayers, music and environment on the crystalline structure of water. Dr Emoto has been freezing different samples of water droplets and then photographing them using an extremely accurate microscope. The water that was exposed to positive words and phrases turned out to be clearly more pleasant looking under the microscope than the one that was exposed to negative comments.

We also watched some people trying out the same experiment using cooked rice in jars, labelling the first jar with Love, second with Hate and third without labels as a control sample. For 6 to 8 weeks, every day, the person would say love and positive words to the 'Love' jar, hateful words to the 'Hate' jar and not a word to the control sample. The results were miraculous. After several weeks, the rice in the 'Hate' jar started looking more rotten and black. The control jar developed mould also but not as strong as the 'Hate' jar. Whilst the 'Love' jar was however intact with no moulds but only turned a bit brown. Absolutely mind-blowing.

Adam said, "If only we had 6 weeks with you grandpa, we could have tried that experiment together."

Milly encouraged him to try it at home with his little brother, adding, "Now you know why I am fascinated by water, as they say in Native American Lakota language, *Mni Wiconi,* which means water is life."

Ty was still puzzled trying to digest what he just saw on television. He looked gently to Milly and asked, "If water has memory and can change shape based on people's emotions, does that mean we get affected too when we drink the water?"

Milly nodded saying, "Since human bodies are made out of 75% to 85% water, we really need to be kind with our words to each other and even towards the food and water that we consume."

We agreed, and Nayyirah added, "Just imagine! Every word that comes out of your mouth can positively or negatively affect the plants in the room!" Milly and Adam giggled. I laughed too. "Yep, from now on, we will definitely have to think carefully before we say a word, or else the plants will stop growing."

It was such an eye-opener to learn more about water and to be considerate to our surroundings, not only spreading kindness towards humans, but also animals and every other living thing in the universe. I found my grandchildren's response to this film so moving and inspirational.

NOTE TO SELF: Kindness is a form of intelligence that benefits everyone and everything in the entire universe. Feeding your mind with useful and positive resources is also an act of kindness to yourself and others.

COMMUNITY MATTERS

At the same time every year, I take my grandchildren to the neighbourhood Community Day. We get to bake cakes, cook hot nutritious meals and share the food with homeless people in the area.

Today, we all split up for a while to walk the streets and talk to the homeless, listen to their stories and share a meal with them. While I was walking, I saw Nayyirah and Ty spending a lot of time with one lady, not really engaging with the other families. I waved at them, hoping they would remember what we had spoken about in the car on the way over — to socialise with as many people as possible, but stay nearby. They waved back at me and then disappeared around the corner with the woman. I was bothered, thinking to myself they must have forgotten.

Adam, Milly and myself soon ended up in the community hall where we were reunited with the rest of our neighbours. "How is it going?" I asked them. "I hope you were able to put smiles on people's faces." The two of them smiled back at me, nodding.

Just then Nayyirah and Ty appeared and started walking towards us.

"Grandpa Hadid, we had a great time talking to different people," Ty said proudly. "We even offered to help a lady out with an issue she was having. Just like you taught me on Tuesday!"

While I was telling them how happy I was to hear that, Nayyirah came in and handed me a recycled carton box that had a small hole on both sides.

"This is a gift to remind you of us and to thank you for all that you do for the community," she said.

I slowly opened the box to find two adorable kittens staring up at me with big, trusting eyes. With tears in my eyes, I instantly fell in love with them.

One of the kittens had a healing cut on her head. It turns out that the lady Nayyirah and Ty were talking to had kittens that needed a loving home as the stray cats were being aggressive around them.

"Right, that makes sense now!" I said. "That's why you both disappeared when I waved at you earlier!"

She smiled. "Yes. I didn't want you to know. You were the first person that came to mind when she told us, Grandpa. You'd be a great grandpa to these kittens too!"

The children laughed when she said that, and my heart swelled with happiness.

Today was one of the best days I've ever had. It was such a great reminder of how fulfilling it is to give back to the community. It's so easy to get carried away with our daily lives and forget to lend a helping hand to those in need. My sweet kittens — who I have named Salt and Pepper — will always remind me of that.

NOTE TO SELF: There is more than one way to show kindness and give back to the community. It could be as simple as smiling at someone. Just open your heart and take the first step towards helping others.

KEY TO LIFE

I always dread the last day of our vacation together. The worst part is saying goodbye to the children when their parents, guardians and family members come to pick them up.

I usually give the children small gifts when they leave to remind them of their time with me. This year, I gifted them small pots of soil and packets of seeds that they can plant at home and watch grow. Believe it or not, it was Adam's idea, with Ty's help, as they were inspired after watching the documentaries about the water. They seemed to appreciate the gesture and promised to share pictures of the plants' progress weekly.

The biggest surprise when I saw the gift that the children gave me — a box of six white plates — they said it's for next visit. All thanks to our neighbour who helped them with purchasing it online.

Ty who — if you remember — was not keen to be spending the week with us, seemed upset to be leaving. He looked at me with teary eyes and said, "Thank you for having us this week, Grandpa Hadid, I will really miss spending time with you, Nayyirah, Adam and Milly," adding, "I can't wait for next year's escapade with you all."

It was hard to let go when I gave each one their last hug of the trip. They all got in their rides, waving at me with mixed emotions showing on their little faces. I will admit that I shed a few tears when their cars were out of sight.

This week was so special to me — to all of us, I think and as much as it saddened me to see my grandchildren leaving today, I was equally happy that they were on their way to their next adventure. Who knows what might happen over the next year? I can't wait to hear all about it.

A big part of me has been inspired by my grandchildren's subtle acts of kindness and the pure compassion and care they showed me throughout their stay. Compassion and kindness seems to come to children much more naturally than it does to adults, which is why I think it's so important to practise those things when one is young.

On top of magical memories, I also gained two companions. Salt and Pepper, my kittens, are wonderful reminders of my grandchildren and their blossoming kindness.

NOTE TO SELF: Kindness is key to making us better human beings.

About the Author

Yasmine is always in boundless search of ways to make this world a kinder, more peaceful place for this and future generations. From adopting quirky homeless cats to instilling the benefits of meditation in her home, she aims to surround her two daughters and their motley crew with different acts of compassion and kindness every day.

Along her journey, she has come to discover the abundant benefits of the passion she now shares with her children. It is in this spirit that Yasmine writes — to share, to inspire and to motivate.

A self-confessed learner, her future plans include starting a foundation to support the education of less fortunate children, keeping her daily gratitude journal brimming with appreciation and continuing her path of enlightenment.